SCHOLASTIC

Let's Find Out

My REBUS Reader

I0890043

How Do Animals Say I Love You?

by Karan Henry

SCHOLASTIC INC.
New York Toronto London Auckland Sydney New Delhi Hong Kong

The  lick.

dogs

The   hug.

orangutans

The  play.

bears

The  nibble.

horses

The  kiss.

prairie dogs

The  nuzzle.

lions

Try saying it in sign language.

How do you say **I love you**?